To:

....

From:

....

Date:

....

ALSO BY ANNIE F. DOWNS

For Kids

What Sounds Fun to You?

Perfectly Unique

Speak Love

Looking for Lovely (for teen girls)

For Adults

That Sounds Fun

100 Days to Brave

Let's All Be Brave

Remember God

Looking for Lovely

100 DAYS
to brave
FOR KiDS

Devotions for Overcoming Fear
and Finding Your Courage

New York Times bestselling author
ANNIE F. DOWNS

ZONDER**kidz**

ZONDERKIDZ

100 Days to Brave for Kids
Copyright © 2022 by Annie F. Downs

Requests for information should be addressed to:
Zonderkidz, *3900 Sparks Dr. SE, Grand Rapids, Michigan 49546*

ISBN 978-0-310-75121-2 (hardcover)
ISBN 978-0-310-75163-2 (audio)
ISBN 978-0-310-75160-1 (ebook)

The author is represented by Alive Literary Agency, www.aliveliterary.com.

Zonderkidz is a trademark of Zondervan.

Zondervan titles may be purchased in bulk for educational, business, fundraising, or sales promotional use. For information, please email SpecialMarkets@Zondervan.com.

Cover Design: Micah Kandros
Interior Design: Denise Froehlich

Printed in Korea

22 23 24 25 26 / SAMWHA / 10 9 8 7 6 5 4 3 2 1

For Ben, Zanna, and Sam

INTRODUCTION

*H*i, friend!

My name is Annie, and before you even get started, I want you to know I think you are brave. You can probably tell me a few brave moments you've had in your life—and I bet there will be a lot more! This book is not about making you brave, it's about showing you how brave you already are.

So for one hundred days, we are going to talk about what those other brave times might look like, how to notice them, and how to be ready for them so you can become even braver in the future. These one hundred days are special to me, and I hope they will be to you as well. I've pulled together some of my favorite thoughts on courage and bravery and wrote them especially with you in mind. And I think that together with whatever God is already doing in your life, this could be a really interesting journey for you.

I know I'm not REALLY there with you as you read, but in my heart it kinda feels like I am! Just think of me as your friend across the kitchen table or on the playground, or someone just hanging out and talking about being brave. I'm cheering for you!

Sincerely,

brave KiDS
HAVE TO START
SOMEWHERE!

WHAT IS BRAVE?

"For I am the LORD your God who takes hold of your right hand and says to you, Do not fear; I will help you."

—ISAIAH 41:13 NIV

Being brave isn't something that happens when you're not scared anymore. I bet you have felt scared sometimes—me too! Whether it is a thunderstorm or a loud dog barking, or you want to try something new and you're worried you may fail, life can feel scary. And we want those scary things to go away, don't we? Sometimes fear even whispers in your mind, telling you that you aren't good enough or smart enough or strong enough to really be brave. We don't stop hearing the whispers of fear—those usually stick around. But brave kids hear those whispers and take action anyway. Sometimes we have to do things even while we're still a little afraid. Being brave is hearing that voice of fear in your head and saying, "Okay, but the truth is, God made me on purpose and for a purpose. So I can do this. I have everything I need to be brave!"

Why do you want to be brave?

....
....
....
....
....
....
....
....

> For the next one hundred days, I want to show you that you are braver than you know.

....
....
....
....
....

You can do this!

Day 2

WHY BE BRAVE?

We can only keep on going, after all, by the power of God, who first saved us and then called us to this holy work. We had nothing to do with it. It was all *his* idea, a gift prepared for us in Jesus long before we knew anything about it. But we know it now.

—2 TIMOTHY 1:8–9 MSG

It is scary to be who you're meant to be. It doesn't feel easy, because it's not. But we were made for this. Like today's scripture says, we have holy work to do. Why be brave? Because when we're brave enough to share the God stories in our lives, it changes the people around us. Remember when you saw that friend from the neighborhood go ALL THE WAY across the monkey bars for the first time and then you thought you could maybe do that too? Seeing other people be brave makes us want to be brave as well. It's a domino effect. It is like confetti at a party or snowflakes falling from the sky. When you are brave, it gets on everyone around you and helps them feel braver. And it changes YOU too!

We want to be brave because we want to be exactly who God made us to be, live the story He has for our lives, and not miss out on any good thing because of fear.

What's your God story? How has God changed you and the things that have happened in your life and made them better?

....
....
....
....
....
....
....

> We have to be brave so that others will be inspired to be brave along with us.

....
....
....
....

Show everyone you are brave!

Day 3

YOU ARE BRAVER THAN YOU KNOW

Whether you turn to the right or to the left, your ears will hear a voice behind you, saying, "This is the way; walk in it."

—ISAIAH 30:21 NIV

If you and I sat down and you told me your story, I bet I would be able to show you times when you made really brave choices, even if you don't label them that way. You're probably already doing more brave things than you realize. You are braver than you know. Brave kids have stories to tell, and in those stories, you are already making big, brave decisions that are making a difference in the lives around you. You need to remember that you are already brave—God MADE you that way. You may not always feel brave, but you are.

What have you done before that made you feel brave?

....

....

....

....

....

....

....

....

....

....

....

....

....

....

....

Friend, you need to know this. I never *felt* brave. I just did the next thing.

You are braver than you know.

Day 4

LOOK FOR BRAVE

The officials were amazed to see how brave Peter and John were, and they knew that these two apostles were only ordinary men and not well educated. The officials were certain that these men had been with Jesus.

—ACTS 4:13 CEV

It's pretty fun to see other friends being brave. Or your parents or favorite grown-up doing something brave—that's cool too. There is something superpowerful about putting brave on display—in your life, in the lives of the people you love, even sometimes in the books you read or the shows you watch! When we see brave out in the world, it inspires us, doesn't it? I think that's why we not only need to share our brave, but we need to actively look for it as well. So, I've got a little challenge for you today! Your job today is to look for someone else doing something brave. It doesn't have to be big; it can be something pretty normal, because sometimes normal is brave too.

Do you see a friend or a family member being brave today?

....
....
....
....
....
....

When you hear other stories, they will sound like your story, and you will realize you are braver than you give yourself credit for.

....
....
....
....
....

Where do you see brave moments in your own life?

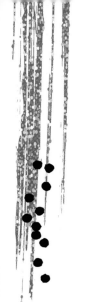

Day 5

JUST START

Saul said to David, "Go, and the LORD be with you."

—1 SAMUEL 17:37 NIV

It can feel hard to just START. Start reading a book, start throwing a football, start singing a song. To start the journey toward that thing—whatever it is for you—is not a journey *to* courage. The moment you take that first step, the moment you start, little seeds of courage—the ones I believe are already planted there right now—begin to sprout in your heart. You are brave before you start, but once you start? You feel the brave grow in you!

What brave thing are you journeying toward? Maybe it's something you long to create, write, say, or do. Take a few minutes to write about it.

....
....
....
....
....
....
....
....

You aren't headed out to find courage. It's in you; it is blooming.

....
....
....
....
....
....

Courage is with you as you say yes to things that seem scary.

Day 6

>>>———————>

THE LIES YOU BELIEVE

And the woman said to the serpent, "We may eat of the fruit
of the trees in the garden, but God said, 'You shall not eat of
the fruit of the tree that is in the midst of the garden, neither
shall you touch it, lest you die.'" But the serpent said to the
woman, "You will not surely die."

—GENESIS 3:2–4 ESV

*E*verything you use in your house has a label—the soap, the crackers,
even your clothes! And when friends say unkind words about you,
sometimes that can feel like a label too—like it is stuck to you. For
example, you get called a name that isn't true about you, but you believe
it. You treat it like truth, and it begins to define you, like a label. It sticks
in your brain and your heart even though it is a lie! It's a vicious cycle
that can only be stopped by a heaping dose of truth—the real stuff.

20

That's why I love the Bible. In His Word, God has already given us all the labels we need, and that's how we learn how to treat ourselves and each other.

Read the words below—these are labels that God has given you! It even says so in the Bible. I wonder if you can find another God-given label in the Bible and add it to the list. What do these labels mean to you?

- Chosen (1 Peter 2:9)
- Forgiven (Colossians 1:13–14)
- Loved (John 3:16)
- Saved (Ephesians 2:8–9)

> It's time to stop listening to Satan's lies and labels so you can hear the truth.

God has already given you all the labels you need.

Day 7

THE TRUTH SETS YOU FREE

Jesus answered, "It is written: 'Man shall not live on bread alone, but on every word that comes from the mouth of God.'"

—MATTHEW 4:4 NIV

The labels that are true about you are very important. And powerful! You are who God says you are, not who other people say you are or who you believe you are. And believing God's truth is always a choice. In every situation, in every conversation, and in every moment when you begin to think less of yourself or forget all the good things God has said about you, you have to fight for truth. Don't give in to the lies!

Is there a name someone has called you that isn't true? Is there a way someone else's words are keeping you from being brave?

....

....

....

....

....

....

....

....

....

....

My insecurities are quieter, my worries are lighter, and my heart is fuller because I know how God feels about me.

....

....

....

....

....

....

The truth that sets you free is God's Word.

Day 8

>>>>————

YOU ARE NOT
A MISTAKE

I praise you, for I am fearfully and wonderfully made.
Wonderful are your works; my soul knows it very well.

—PSALM 139:14 ESV

believe in the me God made (I believe in the you He made too!) and in the me God can make (and I believe He is still making you!). God doesn't make mistakes—not when He made me or when He made you. I believe He made me on purpose and didn't make any mistakes when it came to my creation. That makes me feel brave. And that is the place where I find my courage—knowing that, while I may make mistakes, I am not a mistake. That is where you can find your courage too!

Describe the you that God made. What are three of your best qualities?
What is your favorite talent or ability?

....
....
....
....
....
....
....
....
....

> We can be confident in how God made us because His Word says we are fearfully and wonderfully made.

....
....
....
....
....
....
....

God doesn't make mistakes.

Day 9

YOUR HEART

But you, Lord, are a compassionate and gracious God,
slow to anger, abounding in love and faithfulness.

—PSALM 86:15 NIV

Can you feel your heart beating? Your heart matters—the one you can feel inside you and the place where love lives. Allow God into your heart. Let Him into those little places inside that feel hurt and alone and afraid. It's okay to feel those things, just don't feel them alone in your heart—let God love you, lead you, and make you into the courageous person He has planned. Because I promise that the adventure He has planned for you will be the greatest of your life.

Part of letting God love you is letting Him know you. Talk honestly with Him about your hurts, fears, dreams, and desires.

....

....

....

....

....

....

....

....

....

....

....

....

....

....

....

....

....

....

....

Our God is full of love for you—no matter what you have done or where you have been.

God loves to love you.

Day 10

>>>>———————→

YOUR FEET

Whoever says he abides in [Jesus] ought to walk in the
same way in which he walked.

—1 JOHN 2:6 ESV

Look down at your feet—think of all the places your feet and legs help
you go and the ways they lead you. Even if you're in a wheelchair
or have a hard time walking or running, you can be a great leader!
One of the truest ways to glorify God with your feet is to lead. In fact,
we all have spiritual feet too—a part of us that can lead other people in
good directions. Lead people toward a real relationship with a real God
by how you treat them and the stories you tell. Lead people away from
sin and choices that cause pain. Lead people with the way you live and
how you love and show kindness.

Everyone leads someone. Can you make a list of people who may look up to you as a leader? How can you lead them toward God?

No matter how you're wired, using your feet to lead people takes bravery.

Let your feet lead you down
the path God has for you.

Day 11

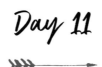

YOUR MIND

Don't be like the people of this world, but let God
change the way you think. Then you will know how to
do everything that is good and pleasing to him.

—ROMANS 12:2 CEV

*P*icture your mind—your brain—as a container. It holds a lot of important stuff! So being brave means being sure to protect it. What are the ways that information gets into your mind? Through your eyes and your ears! Those are the places you need to guard and protect. What you hear and what you see will affect your brain (and heart) greatly.

How can you protect the doorways of your mind every day?

....

....

....

....

....

....

....

....

....

....

Everything in the body depends
on the working of the mind.

....

....

....

....

....

....

Be brave enough to protect your mind.

Day 12

SPEAK KINDLY TO YOURSELF

The tongue has the power of life and death, and those who love it will eat its fruit.

—PROVERBS 18:21 NIV

Friend, I bet there are times when you say mean things to yourself or about yourself. It's time to stop! Seriously. God doesn't make mistakes, remember? If you are going to be the person who does the brave things God is calling you to do, you need to use your words to speak life, to speak good and true things, and to speak beautiful things into others. It starts with doing that for yourself. Kind words have power, and if you believe them, you will be brave.

When you look in the mirror, do you think things that build you up or things that leave you feeling unloved and afraid? Write down three kind things to say to yourself, then say them out loud in front of a mirror.

> Speak kindly to yourself, just like Jesus speaks kindly to you.

Speaking kindly to yourself will make you brave.

Day 13

LIKE WHAT YOU LIKE

For the Spirit God gave us does not make us timid, but gives us power, love and self-discipline.

—2 TIMOTHY 1:7 NIV

You know what's brave? LIKING STUFF! No, really! It takes courage to know what you like and really like it, even when your friends say it isn't cool. Give yourself permission to do the thing you want to do, to like whatever *you* want to like. That's my hope for you. That as you grow to love yourself more and more, you will feel brave enough to love the things you love—sports or instruments or dance or books—instead of changing things because you want to be accepted by your friends. It takes courage, but it makes for a way better life!

What do you really like? What's your favorite way to relax? What type of music do you love? Make a list of five of your favorite things!

....
....
....
....
....
....
....

You are accepted by God. And hopefully you accept you too.

....
....
....
....
....
....

You can like anything you want to like.

Day 14

>>>> ———————→

GOD MADE YOU
ON PURPOSE

The LORD will fulfill his purpose for me; your steadfast love, O LORD, endures forever. Do not forsake the work of your hands.

—PSALM 138:8 ESV

God made you one time. Just once. There is no one just like you! You were worth the work that first time. Then He threw away that mold because one of you is enough for Him. You're enough. You are THE original YOU. Your skin color and your body and your fingers and toes and heart—all of you! God made you this way on purpose, and He created you for His glory. Giving God glory is like shining a spotlight on how awesome He is. And the fact that He made you uniquely awesome shows how amazing He is.

List a few ways you—unique, original, one-of-a-kind you—can live for God's glory this week.

....
....
....
....
....
....

> When God made you, He did something that only He can do, and He did that for His glory.

....
....
....
....
....

Your call to courage is as unique as you are.

brave KiDS

BELIEVE WHAT GOD SAYS!

Day 15

>>>> ———→

ASK THE HARD
QUESTIONS

"Call to me and I will answer you and tell you great
and unsearchable things you do not know."

—JEREMIAH 33:3 NIV

It takes bravery to ask the hard questions and listen for hard answers, no matter who you are talking with—your family or friends or a teacher. Even God! Whatever the hard question is, you can ask. Even if and when things are hard, you can always ask God, "What's Your plan for me? What am I supposed to be learning right now?" He will show you the answer. And those answers, my friend? They are the answers that bring peace to your heart and help you in a lot of ways.

What hard question is on your heart right now?

....

....

....

....

....

....

....

....

Knowing that God works for your
good and that His answers can
be trusted is a great cure for fear.

....

....

....

....

....

....

*Don't be afraid to ask God the
things you really want to know.*

Day 16

>>>———→

BELIEVE YOU ARE
NEVER ALONE

"And surely I am with you always, to the very end of
the age."

—MATTHEW 28:20 NIV

*D*o you know what *Immanuel* means? It is one of God's names, and it means "God with us." Because Jesus paid the price for our sin, God is always with us. See? Even when you feel alone, you actually aren't. He is the One who sticks with you no matter what. And you are brave enough to believe that what He said is true. He is always with you.

Describe one time in your life when you knew God was with you.

....

....

....

....

....

....

....

....

....   Do the hard thing God
                                                                            is leading you to do.
....   You are never alone.

....

....

....

....

....

Jesus said He would be with
us until the end of time.

Day 17

>>>───────→

DIG INTO GOD'S WORD
FOR YOURSELF

Every part of Scripture is God-breathed and useful
one way or another—showing us truth, exposing our
rebellion, correcting our mistakes, training us to live
God's way. Through the Word we are put together and
shaped up for the tasks God has for us.

—2 TIMOTHY 3:16–17 MSG

*W*ould it feel helpful to hear from God when you have to be brave? Well, you can! The Bible is always your best resource when you want to hear from God. There, in black and white (and sometimes red), are God-inspired words for you. You don't have to wait for someone else to tell you what it says (once you've learned how to read) because God's Word is for you too! Dig into the Word for yourself and enjoy this gift God has given you—total access to who He is and total knowledge of how He feels about you!

How do you feel about the Bible? Do you ever read it on your own? What is your favorite verse?

....

....

....

....

....

....

....

....

....

....

....

....

....

> The Bible is God's way of communicating with you, of letting you in on who He is.

The Bible is a record of who God is and His great love for His people.

Day 18

>>>>————

PRAY

This is the confidence we have in approaching God: that
if we ask anything according to his will, he hears us.

—1 JOHN 5:14 NIV

God loves when we pray to Him. And your prayers change things!
No matter your age, God is listening when you pray. Are you
brave enough to pray and believe that God hears you? Are you
brave enough to believe with your whole heart that God will do something miraculous? (Miracles still happen today—all the time!) But really,
prayer isn't about us. Prayer is this amazing opportunity to connect
directly with God, the greatest Being who has always been and the One
who loves you so, so much. Talking with Him and listening to Him can
be the best parts of your day!

What is something you have been praying for? Take your desire to God, and be brave enough to believe He can do anything, even what seems impossible.

....

....

....

....

....

....

....

....

God is absolutely real.
And He is listening.

....

....

....

....

....

It takes courage to connect with God through prayer.

Day 19

HAVE FAITH

Now faith is confidence in what we hope for and assurance about what we do not see.

—HEBREWS 11:1 NIV

When you have a hard day, when something goes sideways and you feel mad and sad and maybe you even doubt God's Word or God's love for you, what's your first brave move? Hold up the shield of faith that you hold over your heart. Just believe. Choose to believe that God is good and God is kind (as well as a bunch of other things brave kids believe about God, which we'll list in just a few days!), but remember it may not feel all that different right at first. Feeling isn't believing. Believing is deeper than that. It isn't always easy to believe—in fact, it rarely is—but the good stuff is never easy. And what happens to your soul on the other side of a fight for faith is the good stuff.

What are some words you would use to describe how it feels to BELIEVE even when you can't see what God is doing?

....

....

....

....

....

....

....

| Ask God to fill you with faith—faith in Him, faith in His promises, faith in His ways. |

....

....

....

....

....

....

When you ask God to increase your faith, He will.

Day 20

>>>>——————————>

GOD IS WHO HE
SAYS HE IS

God is not human, that he should lie, not a human
being, that he should change his mind. Does he speak
and then not act? Does he promise and not fulfill?

—NUMBERS 23:19 NIV

You are deeply loved and called to be courageous by a God who is perfect and perfectly trustworthy. If you feel stuck when you look at your own shortcomings, look upward to your Jesus, who is exactly who He says He is. He defeated death itself, and He empowers you to be brave.

Romans 8:11 says you are empowered by the same Spirit who lived in Jesus. How does that help you to feel brave?

....
....
....
....
....
....

....

....

....

Instead of looking at yourself and your own abilities, look at God and believe that He is who He says He is.

....
....
....
....
....

God is making you brave day by day.

Day 21

>»»> ———→

YOU CAN HEAR GOD

"The shepherd walks right up to the gate. The
gatekeeper opens the gate to him and the sheep
recognize his voice. He calls his own sheep by name
and leads them out. When he gets them all out, he
leads them and they follow because they are familiar
with his voice."

—JOHN 10:2–4 MSG

Some people say God doesn't speak to us anymore, but I don't
believe that at all! I think He is always speaking to us—through
the Bible and through nature, like the birds singing and the seasons changing. He speaks through others—our parents, teachers, or
friends—through Jesus's life, and directly through the Holy Spirit, who

lives in us. You can hear Him too, if you want to. God wants to talk to you—you are never too young to talk to God and hear Him for yourself!

What would you like to hear from God right now?

....

....

....

....

....

....

....

....

....

....

....

....

....

....

> I have learned to hear God's voice in my life. I know that quiet voice and that gentle push.

Take a deep breath and learn to hear God's voice in your life.

Day 22

YOU ARE WHO GOD SAYS YOU ARE

Therefore, as God's chosen people, holy and dearly loved, clothe yourselves with compassion, kindness, humility, gentleness and patience.

—COLOSSIANS 3:12 NIV

A lot of people will try to tell you who you are—remember we talked about those labels? Well, one of the best parts of spending time with God (by praying to Him and listening to Him) is you get to hear over and over who you REALLY are. When you spend time with God and really listen to the truth of His Word, you will easily notice the lies and the things you hear in your head that aren't really you. You will hear the truth of who God says you are much more clearly, like how you are dearly loved.

Who does God say you are?

....

....

....

....

....

....

....

....

....

> All over His Word, God says that you are strong and important on this planet.

....

....

....

....

....

You are accepted. You are secure. You can be brave.

Day 23

>>>———→

BELIEVE GOD CARES
ABOUT YOUR DREAMS

"If you, then, though you are evil, know how to give
good gifts to your children, how much more will your
Father in heaven give good gifts to those who ask him!"

—MATTHEW 7:11 NIV

W hile I do really think God cares about the things you dream at
night, that's not what I'm talking about here. I'm talking about
the hopes and dreams you have for your life—what you want
to do and be when you grow up and are an adult. Some people have big
dreams for their future and some of us are still figuring it out—both are
okay! But it's important for you to pay attention to your dreams because
your life and your dreams are important to God. So share your dreams

with your heavenly Father, who loves you and loves to give you good gifts to help you become the person you are meant to be.

What good gifts has God already given you? What do you want that you don't yet have?

....

....

....

....

....

....

> God hears us when we pray. He cares about you, and He cares about your dreams.

....

....

....

....

....

Dream and believe that God is working in those dreams.

Day 24

>>>>————————→

GOD IS LOVING

For God so loved the world that he gave his one and only Son, that whoever believes in him shall not perish but have eternal life.

—JOHN 3:16 NIV

It's really important for brave kids to know and believe that God is loving. You have to know God's character as you are taking brave steps in life. And He is really loving. You are so loved right now, and right where you are, more than you can imagine. But try to think about how big that love is. Try to think about what it would feel like, in your heart and mind and belly, to be loved without any worries. Because you are! That's you! That's God! That's y'all together! You can't run away from His love or jump out of His grasp. He's got you! He loves you so much!

How does believing that God is loving make you more brave?

....

....

....

....

....

....

....

....

....

You are one of a kind, made on purpose, deeply loved, and called to be courageous.

....

....

....

....

....

....

....

God loves you so much!

Day 25

>>>> ———➤

GOD IS FORGIVING

In him we have redemption through his blood, the
forgiveness of sins, in accordance with the riches of
God's grace that he lavished on us.

—EPHESIANS 1:7–8 NIV

I said something unkind to a friend last week. It made me sad that I
hurt her feelings and I felt really bad about it. I texted her later and
apologized, saying I was so sorry for what I had said. She wrote back,
"All is forgiven." I thought about that a long time. It feels hard to believe,
doesn't it? ALL is forgiven is A LOT of forgiveness. With humans, those
words can be just words. But with God, we know they are really, really
true! No matter what you do, you never have to earn God's love or get
on His good side—when you make a mistake and ask for forgiveness,
He gives it all!

Why is forgiveness important to you? Can you remember the last time someone had to forgive you or you had to forgive someone else?

....
....
....
....
....
....
....
....
....

> Over and over again, I ask Jesus for forgiveness and rescue, and He always provides them.

....
....
....
....
....
....

You are forgiven!

Day 26

GOD IS KIND

Change your life, not just your clothes. Come back
to God, *your* God. And here's why: God is kind and
merciful. He takes a deep breath, puts up with a lot, this
most patient God, extravagant in love, always ready to
cancel catastrophe.

—JOEL 2:13 MSG

Is God really kind? That feels like a hard question when our lives don't
always seem to work out so easy. You are making a brave choice when
you look past your circumstances and choose to believe that God is
who He says He is. The good days and the bad days of your life don't tell
us who God is. Because God never changes—He is the same yesterday,
today, and always! And He is also kind. You can see it in nature and in

the people who love you and in all the Bible stories—you may not see it or understand it right now, but God is always being kind to you!

What does it look like to be kind to someone else? When have you noticed God's kindness in your own life?

....
....
....
....
....
....
....
....
....
....
....
....

> No matter what, choose to believe that God is kind. You will see that He is.

God's kindness is one of the best things about Him.

Day 27

>>>>———————➤

GOD IS LISTENING

Is anyone crying for help? GOD is listening, ready to rescue you.

—PSALM 34:17 MSG

God is listening. Do you need Him? Do you need help? Do you need a friend? Do you need to talk about some things that are important to you? God is ready to hear them! If it is important to you, it is important to God! There are times when I pray and nothing happens that I can see right away, and there are times when I pray and it feels like God is very close. It will take you being brave, remembering and knowing that He listens, to keep growing your prayer life. Never forget that He is always listening to your prayers and ready to help you!

Do you need God's help? He is listening. Pray right now and ask Him for the help you need!

When someone listens to you, it's because you really matter to them. That's how God feels about you!

God loves to hear from you.

Day 28

>>>>———————>

GOD IS SPEAKING

*"Call to me and I will answer you and tell you great
and unsearchable things you do not know."*

—JEREMIAH 33:3 NIV

Remember a few days ago when we talked about how you can hear God? It's because He is always speaking! Way down deep in your heart, if you listen close, He is whispering to you. Be brave! Keep listening! He is saying important things about how loved you are, how special you are, how He has a big and beautiful plan for your life that will be perfect for you. It may take some time for you to get to know His voice, but when you pray, tell Him you want to hear from Him and then listen really close!

What do you think God sounds like in your life?

God loves to speak to you.

*It's brave to listen to God
and do what He says.*

Day 29

GOD IS MOVING IN YOUR LIFE

He says, "Be still, and know that I am God."

—PSALM 46:10 NIV

*D*o you sometimes feel like God isn't at work in your life? It feels like that in my life too. We pray and we hope, but it seems like nothing changes. Have you ever asked the question, "God, do You even care?" I have too. Because sometimes it can feel like He isn't moving in our lives.

But the real truth is that He is at work all the time in our lives. It doesn't mean we see all He is doing (in fact, we usually don't), but we believe, by faith, that God is who He says He is and that He will do what He says He will do. And God never stops, never changes, and is always working on our behalf, so even if it feels like everything is standing still, God is working to fill our lives with joy. And people see His work in our stories.

Is there one story in your life where you are trusting God to move things and change things, but you don't see anything yet?

....

....

....

....

....

> We are brave when we believe that God's moving on our behalf. Especially when we can't see it yet.

....

....

....

....

....

God is always working, even when we can't see it.

Day 30

GOD IS IN CONTROL

The LORD has established his throne in heaven, and his kingdom rules over all.

—PSALM 103:19 NIV

It takes a lot of courage to believe that God is always in control. When we see all the hard stuff in the world and we see all that goes wrong in our lives, we may find ourselves asking if God really has this thing under control. And it takes a little bit of extra courage to look at the world around us and believe that God has not lost His spot or His power. Your life may have some sad things going on, or things that make you worry, but remembering God is in control will help you feel safe and peaceful.

Is there an area of your life where knowing that God is in control makes you feel better about the situation?

....
....
....
....
....
....
....
....

God cares about your
life, and He's with you.

....
....
....
....
....
....

*God is in control today
and every day.*

Day 31

GOD IS NEAR

But as for me, it is good to be near God. I have made the Sovereign Lord my refuge; I will tell of all your deeds.

—PSALM 73:28 NIV

*D*oes anyone you love live in a different city? It can be so sad to be away from people you love or have to say goodbye after a visit or a holiday. Some of my family lives far away from me and I wish they were closer! But one of the best things about God is that He is always near to you! When you feel alone, when you are sad or worried, you can be brave and remember that God will never leave you.

Have you ever felt lonely? How has God helped you?

....

....

....

....

....

....

....

....

....

....

Since God is always with you, you can be brave!

....

....

....

....

....

....

Even right now, God is close to you!

Day 32

>>>>————➤

GOD IS JUST

God is just.

—2 THESSALONIANS 1:6 NIV

O ur world seems unfair a lot, doesn't it? Not just in the little things, like someone cheating at a game or your family's car getting a flat tire, but also in very big things too. You've probably heard the word *justice* before, right? It's a word we use for the good guys. They love justice. It means that in the end, while life might not be fair, things will turn out right. God is just, but when we live in a fallen world—a place full of unkind people and unfair stories—it is hard to see God bringing justice. And believing he will is, again, something that takes some courage. Courage to live day in and day out in an unjust world, to do what we can to help our neighbors and friends who have a harder time in life, and still believe that God is just. Nothing slips by Him, nothing is unseen. God will make all things new—it's a promise!

What are some ways you could help your friends and neighbors experience justice in their lives?

....

....

....

....

....

....

....

Life may not feel fair, but God will handle it all for you.

....

....

....

....

....

God sees everything. He is taking care of you and will take care of you.

brave KiDS

DREAM AND
WORK HARD!

Day 33

GOD IS ENOUGH

You, LORD, are my shepherd. I will never be in need.

—PSALM 23:1 CEV

t Christmas, my friends get four kinds of gifts—something they want, something to read, something to wear, and something they need. Maybe your family does the same? Something you really want, a book to read, a new piece of clothing to wear, and one thing that grown-ups think kids need.

We can all think of things we need, right? Whether it's a new pair of socks or a new friend, enough food for dinner or a good night's sleep. We need a lot of things. But God promises over and over in the Bible that He will take care of us, that He is enough. I know that sounds wild, but it's true. We can all find gaps in our lives, places where we have need—kids and grown-ups alike. But are we all brave enough to believe that God is enough to fill them to overflowing? It takes a lot of courage to be in a place where you don't have everything you want and you ask God to be enough. He's a creative God. He can meet your needs in ways you could not even predict. But He will do it if you are brave enough to ask!

What are some needs you have today that you could ask God to meet?

....
....
....
....
....
....　God will take care of you!
....
....
....
....

Tell God what you need and watch Him meet your needs in amazing ways.

Day 34

>>>> ─────

DREAM BIG

And while [Jesus] was at Bethany in the house of Simon the leper, as he was reclining at table, a woman came with an alabaster flask of ointment of pure nard, very costly, and she broke the flask and poured it over his head. There were some who said to themselves indignantly, "Why was the ointment wasted like that? For this ointment could have been sold for more than three hundred denarii and given to the poor." And they scolded her. But Jesus said, "Leave her alone. Why do you trouble her? She has done a beautiful thing to me."

—MARK 14:3–6 ESV

*B*ig dreams are so fun! (And they take a lot of courage!) Be brave enough to believe that as much as you could want, God could give to you. We are meant to make a big impact on the planet. You were born to do something great for God! It doesn't have to be big or loud, it doesn't have to be newsworthy, but God has a great plan for you—more incredible than anything you could ever dream up on your own. It still amazes me how God's dream for me was so much greater than the one I'd been planning all along. So what are you dreaming?

Name someone who's doing big things for God. What impresses you about their story? What's a big thing you want to do for God?

> God loves to put wings on dreams that His kids chase.

Be brave enough to dream big.

Day 35

WHAT'S AN OPEN DOOR?

He leads me in paths of righteousness for his name's
sake.

—PSALM 23:3 ESV

I love when someone opens up a door for me—like a stranger at the post
office or a neighbor helping while I'm bringing in groceries. There are
also open doors with God. When I was a sophomore in college, I knew
I wanted to go on a mission trip—a trip to another country to serve the
people there and share about God, and of the list of trips our church was
offering, the one to Scotland stood out to me. It was an open door. It's
important to pay attention to opportunities—whether it is an invitation
to go on a trip or be on a sports team or try out for a musical or play, or
answer questions about your life with God. Going on a trip overseas,
and later going to live in Scotland, took courage. It was different. It was

new. And I wasn't following a path lit with bright, glowing arrows on the ground. It was an open door that God led me through. Ask the Lord to lead *you* to the doors He is opening for you, then be brave enough to walk through them.

When has God opened a door for you? What came of that opportunity? What door would you like to see Him open for you now?

....

....

....

....

....

....

How do you know when to make a brave move, even if it isn't easy?

....

....

....

....

Ask God to show you the open doors in your life right now.

Day 36

WHAT'S A CLOSED DOOR?

Commit to the LORD whatever you do, and he will
establish your plans.

—PROVERBS 16:3 NIV

Just like open doors are important to watch for, closed doors
are too. Yes, they can be really disappointing—but they matter.
Whether you don't make the team or you lose the spelling bee or
you have to move to a new school or town, when you lose something or
see a door closed, pay attention! Another door is about to open! That's
because if you're looking at a closed door today, there's an open one
just around the corner. Brave kids trust God's plan for their lives, even
though it might not look the way they thought it would. Be brave enough
to walk through the doors that the Lord leads you through. Even when

they are unexpected or feel scary. And be brave enough to trust Him when He closes a door.

When has God closed a door for you? What came of it—did you adjust your plan or wait for an open door?

....

....

....

....

....

....

Closed doors can be confusing. But when they happen, you can be brave.

....

....

....

....

....

....

You can be brave because you can trust God.

Day 37

TELL SOMEONE

And let us consider how we may spur one another on toward love and good deeds, not giving up meeting together, as some are in the habit of doing, but encouraging one another—and all the more as you see the Day approaching.

—HEBREWS 10:24–25 NIV

Think about the dreams you have for your life. Have you shared them with anyone? Your dreams aren't silly or impossible! So don't worry about telling someone else—people want to help you and would love to hear about your dreams. I bet some of your favorite grown-ups would love to know what you are dreaming for your future. Maybe someone can help you really make a plan and think through what you hope God has planned for your life?

Think about a dream (maybe there's more than one) that's alive in you today. What questions or fears do you have? What obstacles stand in your way? How will you tell people about this dream?

....

....

....

....

....

....

Tell somebody you want to be brave, and then see what God can do.

....

....

....

....

....

....

Do you want to be brave?
Tell someone.

Day 38

HOW DO YOU FIND THE PEOPLE TO TELL?

Without good direction, people lose their way; the
more wise counsel you follow, the better your chances.

—PROVERBS 11:14 MSG

Telling the right person about your dreams is very, very important!
Your dreams live in your heart and brain, so inviting friends and
family in to hear about them is such a special thing. And your heart
is precious, which means your dreams should be shared with only a few
close people. Be a little careful—brave kids share what is on their hearts
with people they trust, so make sure you are trusting people who are
loving and safe. Your dreams matter, and telling the right people will
help you be brave so you can make these dreams come true!

Can you name one friend and one grown-up that you would trust to tell your big dreams to?

....

....

....

....

....

....

....

Wise people live wise lives. Find them. Watch for them. And then keep them around your life.

....

....

....

....

....

....

....

Brave kids share what is on their hearts with people they trust.

Day 39

>>>> ———→

WHAT WERE YOU
CREATED TO DO?

Jesus said, 'Love the Lord your God with all your passion
and prayer and intelligence.' This is the most important,
the first on any list. But there is a second to set alongside
it: 'Love others as well as you love yourself.'

—MATTHEW 22:37-39 MSG

*D*o you ever wonder why you were born? Do you think about why
you're here on this earth? No person is an accident, so if God
made you on purpose, what were you created to do? We know, as
Christians, that we are all called to point people to Christ. To love God,
and to love others as we love ourselves. But how are you supposed to

do that practically, using your unique personality and gifts? Ask God. Spend time in His Word. God is always speaking to us.

What parts of you feel created for a purpose? Ask God now to show you how to live out your calling with those gifts. Ask Him now to show you how to live out your calling. Then wait, listen, and journal what you hear.

....

....

....

....

....

One thing we know for sure is that it is brave to love God and love others.

....

....

....

....

The best way to grow in your ability to hear God is to practice and let others help you.

Day 40

>>>———→

WORK HARD

Hard work always pays off; mere talk puts no bread on the table.

—PROVERBS 14:23 MSG

*B*eing a hard worker is a big deal. It's a real sign that you are brave. You gain a lot when you work really hard. You gain respect. You gain a good reputation. It builds muscles—in your body, yes, but also in your heart and mind! It isn't always fun, but don't you want to be a person who is known for working hard? Whatever you're doing and whatever you're asked to do, work hard. It really does pay off.

What are small things you can do every day to gain a good reputation at home or at school?

....

....

....

....

....

....

....

Persevere. Work hard.
Don't be wimpy.

....

....

....

....

....

....

Work hard today, friend, and
see what comes from it.

Day 41

>>>> ———————→

WHO YOU DO LIFE WITH
MATTERS AS MUCH
AS WHAT YOU DO

As iron sharpens iron, so one person sharpens another.

—PROVERBS 27:17 NIV

Playing soccer is fun, but it's better when your friends are on your team. Everyone loves being in the class with the best teacher in your grade. WHO you spend your time with matters as much as HOW you spend your time! Share your life with others! It is always going to be important for you to be brave with the choices and the decisions you make, but having a great team of people around you will help you have even more courage.

Think about your people. What kind of influence do they have on your life?

....
....
....
....
....
....
....

> Don't let going after your dreams and your calling keep you from investing in strong friendships.

....
....
....
....
....

When you're going after your calling, don't abandon the people who matter.

brave **KIDS**

LOVE OTHER
PEOPLE TOO!

Day 42

>»»——►

BRAVE KIDS
NEED PEOPLE

You are better off to have a friend than to be all alone,
because then you will get more enjoyment out of what
you earn. If you fall, your friend can help you up. But if
you fall without having a friend nearby, you are really
in trouble.

—ECCLESIASTES 4:9–10 cev

*W*e all need friends. Most things in life are better shared with
others, including when we feel afraid or lonely. Brave kids
need other brave people in their lives! Maybe it's a parent or a
grown-up in your church or school or family, or maybe it's another kid
your age who is kind and works hard to do the right thing. Friendship

takes work. Friendship takes courage. But friends are worth it! Having someone brave WITH you is so much better!

What relationships in your life have already proven to be worth the effort? Who is your favorite brave friend?

....

....

....

....

....

....

....

| To make brave choices, you have got to have support. |

....

....

....

....

....

As hard as relationships can be, we wouldn't trade them for the world.

Day 43

YOUR FAMILY

Long, long ago he decided to adopt us into his family through Jesus Christ. (What pleasure he took in planning this!) He wanted us to enter into the celebration of his lavish gift-giving by the hand of his beloved Son.

—EPHESIANS 1:5–6 MSG

*B*eing brave in your family means loving your family well even if your family isn't always healthy or kind or doing the right thing. Both kids and grown-ups make mistakes, and the people who see those mistakes up close the MOST are family! But forgiveness in a family is brave and important—it's following the example of God, who lives and breathes forgiveness and grace. It's praying and asking God to help you love your siblings well and love all the humans who make up your family. Pray for the courage to stick with your family and love them as they are, the way God has loved you.

How have you had to be brave in your family? What's the healthiest way to love your family?

....
....
....
....
....

> For many people, loving your family can take more courage than all of your other relationships combined.

....
....
....
....

It's brave to forgive your family members when they mess up. And it's a way to look more like God.

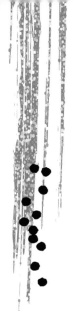

Day 44

>>>>———→

YOUR FRIENDS

Love one another with brotherly affection. Outdo one another in showing honor.

—ROMANS 12:10 ᴇsᴠ

know I sound like a broken record about this, but *you need friends.* But also? THEY NEED YOU. God made us this way—to be together, to cheer for each other, to help each other. When you want to be brave, that includes being brave enough to invite someone new to sit at your lunch table or to try a new sport and introduce yourself to a teammate. Maybe someone has been mean to you before, or made fun of you, and now you wonder if you ever want to have real friends because you've been hurt before. I get that. But courage also means trying again when friendship has been challenging in the past.

Who are two friends that you like talking about brave things with? What about your friends makes you know they are brave?

....
....
....
....
....
....
....

....

I'm so thankful my friends were brave enough to let me into their lives and that I was brave enough to let them into mine.

....

....

....

....

....

Love will change you. It will change your friends.

Day 45

>>>> ⟶

TEACHERS AND COACHES

Trust God from the bottom of your heart; don't try to figure out everything on your own. Listen for God's voice in everything you do, everywhere you go; he's the one who will keep you on track.

—PROVERBS 3:5–6 MSG

Teachers, coaches, and other great grown-ups in your life can certainly help you be braver tomorrow than you are today! Watching how your teacher handles the easy days and the hard days in your classroom, listening to your coach remind your team how important it is to never quit—there are all these little lessons about courage happening in your life every day. Adults are solving problems and making decisions and facing brave choices morning, noon, and night. When you watch them, ask them questions, and get a chance to see how they are doing it, you will learn so much about being brave yourself!

Who are some trusted adults in your life that are brave? What will you tell them next time you see them?

....
....
....
....
....

> You will learn things about God's love and personality from the grown-ups in your life, and that includes teachers and coaches.

....
....
....

Make sure you say a big thanks to your favorite teachers or coaches today!

Day 46

>>>>———

YOUR CHURCH

Love is patient and kind; love does not envy or boast; it is
not arrogant or rude. It does not insist on its own way; it is
not irritable or resentful; it does not rejoice at wrongdoing,
but rejoices with the truth. Love bears all things, believes
all things, hopes all things, endures all things.

—1 CORINTHIANS 13:4–7 ESV

*C*hurch isn't a building, church is a group of people who gather
to worship God—whether that is in a cathedral or a living room
or over the computer. Being a part of a church is really good to
help you grow in your faith. Brave Christians, brave kids who love God,
get plugged in to their church. But just like any relationship, you and
the church will have rocky times. Just like any relationship, at some
point the flawed humans who lead your church will disappoint you,

and you will need to put 1 Corinthians 13 love into action. The leaders and grown-ups will try their best to love like God loves, but we are all human and make mistakes. Do not give up on the church because of the humans involved—love anyway.

Have you been to church before? What's your favorite part?

....

....

....

....

....

....

....

....

....

....

....

> If we unplug from our church, we're unplugging from our support system.

Church gives us the opportunity to wrestle and learn inside so that we can love well outside.

Day 47

>>>───

YOUR ONLINE LIFE

"You are the light of the world. A city set on a hill cannot be hidden. Nor do people light a lamp and put it under a basket, but on a stand, and it gives light to all in the house. In the same way, let your light shine before others, so that they may see your good works and give glory to your Father who is in heaven."

—MATTHEW 5:14–16 ESV

We probably all have smartphones or tablets or laptops in our homes and in our schools and in every part of our lives. There are so many places on the internet where you can talk to people. Make sure you are being safe, and make sure the grown-ups in your life know who you are talking to and what you are searching for. The internet is actually a great place to learn and to share the light of

God! It takes courage to share your faith and be a light for Jesus, whether you're online or not. So be wise, be safe, and be brave with your words about Jesus when you are online!

How are you being a light for Jesus while you're online?

....

....

....

....

....

....

> We are to be a light wherever we go, even online.

....

....

....

....

....

We need to view technology as a tool God gave us to glorify Him.

Day 48

YOUR WORDS MATTER

A word out of your mouth may seem of no account, but
it can accomplish nearly anything—or destroy it!

—JAMES 3:5 MSG

Proverbs 18:21 tells us that our tongues have the power of life and death. What you say REALLY matters! I see that in my life. I see that in my friendships. I see that in the memories of things people said to me a long time ago. Words matter. God wants you to use your words to encourage others and to speak kindly to your friends and family and even strangers. Ask God for the grace to do that, and look for opportunities to be brave, speaking truth and love into a broken world.

What are some ways you can share good words with the people in your life?

....

....

....

....

....

....

....

....

....

....

If there are seeds of courage living in all of us, waiting to bloom, words are the sun and the water that cheer on those seeds to their fullness.

....

....

....

....

....

....

Encouraging words give you the push you need.

Day 49

WHEN RELATIONSHIPS CHANGE

I lift up my eyes to the mountains—where does my help come from? My help comes from the LORD, the Maker of heaven and earth.

—PSALM 121:1-2 NIV

The friendships in your life are going to change over the years. What do you do when things start to change? You lift your eyes up to your Helper. Your Comforter. Your Father. Your Friend. Jesus cares and understands. One of my favorite things about God is that He doesn't change. So when every other relationship changes—as you grow up, as you change classes and schools, maybe when you move to a new neighborhood or church—you can feel sad about that, but also remind yourself that God doesn't change!

What relationships do you see going through a change?

....
....
....
....
....
....

> Every relationship changes. That's a hard reality, one that absolutely requires us to lift our eyes up and let the Lord help.

....
....
....
....
....

When a relationship changes, let the Lord help you through it.

brave KiDS

FACE CHANGE AND
NEVER GIVE UP!

Day 50

>>>> ———➤

CHANGE ALWAYS HAPPENS

Every good and perfect gift is from above, coming down from the Father of the heavenly lights, who does not change like shifting shadows.

—JAMES 1:17 NIV

When I was a kid, I really didn't like change. It felt scary and lonely and unsafe. But life will keep changing—just like the weather. So instead of fearing change, what if we just learned to live with it as part of our lives? You don't have to love it; I still don't love change, but I know that God is always working for my good. So remember that He's the boss and that He loves us. That can make us brave, even when everything that used to feel secure seems to be changing.

What changes in your life are you dreading right now? What changes are you excited about? How is God using these changes to shape you?

....
....
....
....
....
....
....

Brave people are willing to let go of everything as they hold tight to God.

....
....
....
....
....
....

You have a totally trustworthy God who is looking out for you.

Day 51

>>>> ———————

PREPARE FOR CHANGE

Jesus Christ is the same yesterday and today and
forever.

—HEBREWS 13:8 NIV

We can be brave because Jesus is constant, even when our circumstances are not. I need that reminder—that just as the seasons change on earth, they are going to change in my life. And when I start to sense that little bit of shift, like the first hints of fall, that's my chance to prepare and see it coming and know it's all part of the journey. So don't be afraid when change starts happening in your life, in your body, and in your family. Just like winter turns to spring, something really good is going to happen on the other side of this change!

What can you do to prepare for the changes you see coming in the next few days, weeks, or months?

....

....

....

....

....

....

....

....

....

How do you prepare for change? Spend time talking to the unchanging One.

....

....

....

....

....

....

Trust Him, keep your eyes on Him, and let the seasons change.

Day 52

>>>>———————

SMALL DECISIONS MATTER

What a person plants, he will harvest.

—GALATIANS 6:7 MSG

Small decisions don't feel very brave in the moment. When you think of being brave, you probably think of giant leaps. Grand gestures. Those are clearly brave. We usually think it's the really big decisions that change our lives, but often it is the small ones that shape us the most. It's brave to be intentional to make small, healthy decisions every day because those build up and build up and make the big decisions easier. Being brave in how you treat your friends today and how you treat your body today and how you grow in your faith today—in small ways—makes those big-decision days not as scary!

What's one small decision you can make today to be brave and healthy?

It's brave to make
small decisions with
the big picture in mind.

*A little yes can be a step
in the right direction, even
if it isn't a big leap.*

Day 53

SAY YES

The righteous are as bold as a lion.

—PROVERBS 28:1 NIV

SAY YES! You are going to get some chances to try new things and meet new people and you can say YES to those, even if you are a little afraid. If the yeses feel scary, just lean on God! Remember, if you are seeking God, if you are asking Him to lead you, He hears you and is doing just that! If you are living in obedience to Him, and He brings opportunities into your life, you can trust that He will take care of you when you say yes. Don't be afraid to say yes—try new things. Try new foods. Try new activities. Try new friend groups. The more yeses you say, the bigger and better your life will be!

It's often hardest to say yes when something is new. What's something new you can say yes to this week?

....

....

....

....

....

....

....

....

....

....

> Say yes to the situations that stretch you and scare you and ask you to be a better you than you think you can be.

....

....

....

....

....

....

Say yes to Jesus in every way every chance you get.

Day 54

>>>>———

SAY NO

But even if he does not [rescue us], we want you to
know, Your Majesty, that we will not serve your gods or
worship the image of gold you have set up.

—DANIEL 3:18 NIV

*J*ust like you have chances to say YES, you have lots of chances in
life to say NO. Whatever you say YES to today for lunch means
you are saying NO to every other food for this meal, right? A lot of
courageous nos make for some beautifully brave yeses. And I'm not sure
if you are going to get it right every time—saying the right yeses and the
right nos. I don't get it right all the time. But courage doesn't equal right;
courage equals stepping out and trying. Just remember how brave it is
to say no sometimes—when you are pressured to do something wrong,

when you are being bullied or forced, or when saying YES will hurt someone else. Ask God, pray as you go, and He'll help you with the nos.

When is it hard for you to say no?

....

....

....

....

....

....

....

Say the thing that courage asks you to say, even if it's the word *no*.

....

....

....

....

....

Be brave and say yes. But also be brave and say no.

Day 55

WHILE YOU ARE WAITING

Wait for the LORD; be strong, and let your heart take courage; wait for the LORD!

—PSALM 27:14 ESV

*D*o you ever get tired of waiting? Waiting for the school bus, waiting for a show to start, waiting for your turn on the baseball field . . . it is HARD to wait! It actually takes a lot of courage to be patient. When we remember how patient the Lord is with us (He is VERY patient with each of us!), it can help us be patient when we are waiting. Waiting for our hard work to pay off. Waiting for a relationship to heal. Waiting for a bad day to be over. You can be brave in whatever type of waiting you find yourself when you are living in total dependence on your ever-patient, ever-present Father.

When is it the hardest for you to wait?

....

....

....

....

....

....

.... Life is full of waiting seasons,

.... and you can brave out the

.... wait and do it well.

....

....

....

....

....

Be brave enough to be patient not just outwardly but inwardly.

Day 56

WHEN YOU HOLD ON

These hard times are small potatoes compared to the coming good times, the lavish celebration prepared for us. There's far more here than meets the eye. The things we see now are here today, gone tomorrow. But the things we can't see now will last forever.

—2 CORINTHIANS 4:17-18 MSG

When you are dangling from the monkey bars at the playground, it can be really, really hard to hang on. Life's like that too—sometimes holding on and being brave go hand in hand. Another word for holding on is *perseverance*. We want to be brave and not give up when things get hard! Don't let go just because something you're going through hurts or because it is hard. Don't let go because you feel like it is ridiculous to hold on. It's not. Hold on until the Lord makes it really clear that you're supposed to let go of that thing. But while you are listening, persevere, and lean toward holding on until God and other people show you that the time for holding on is done.

Where do you want to quit right now?

....
....
....
....
....
....

> Don't give up on life. Don't give up on God. Don't give up on yourself.

....
....
....
....
....
....

Hold on to hope.

Day 57

WHEN YOU LET GO

"Forget the former things; do not dwell on the past.
See, I am doing a new thing! Now it springs up; do
you not perceive it?"

—ISAIAH 43:18–19 NIV

W hen you move to a new city or a new school, there are some things that are right to let go of, even if it makes you feel sad. Think again about the monkey bars on the playground. The only way you get to grab on to a new one is if you let go of the old one. The same is true when you finish a book or finish a movie—you probably don't want to start the next book in a series until you have finished the one you are reading now! This will happen in life a lot too. So remember it is okay to feel sad when you have to let go of something, and remind yourself it takes a lot of courage to do that. Only in letting go are your hands free to grab on to the next thing.

Do you sense anything you should let go of now?

....

....

....

....

....

....

....

> The deeper call for courage comes when you let go with nothing ahead to grab.

....

....

....

....

....

Be brave enough to empty your hands. You can trust in God!

Day 58

>>>> ———>

WHEN CHANGE HURTS

And we know that in all things God works for the
good of those who love him, who have been called
according to his purpose.

—ROMANS 8:28 NIV

Brave kids are okay with change because they remember that change
is for their good. That doesn't mean you have to love change or
seek change or want change. That doesn't mean that when something takes an unexpected turn, you have to throw a party. It means that
if you're brave, you can walk through change with grace and the hope
that God's promises are true and all things really do work together for
good. A kid who experiences change and gets good at living with change
will become an adult who handles change well. That will be you!

What is one thing you see changing in your life right now?

> A brave person's joy isn't dependent on circumstances. God has got this, whatever it is.

God wants you to live bravely in the knowledge that He is in control.

Day 59

LIFE IS HARD

"I have told you these things, so that in me you may have peace. In this world you will have trouble. But take heart! I have overcome the world."

—JOHN 16:33 NIV

My friend, life is hard. It just is. Jesus said it to us a long time ago—in this world, we will have trouble. I bet you've already experienced that, haven't you? In school or at home or in your family? Life isn't always easy. And yes, you are allowed to feel sad about that. You can also be angry when life is hard. But don't give up, don't worry that life will never be okay again. It will. Even when it gets tragic and dark, do not despair. You are braver than that. Light is coming.

Can you think of one way that life has been hard recently?

....

....

....

....

....

....

....

....

God knows that life is painful.

....

....

....

....

....

....

Tragedy can sneak up on you and send your world into a tailspin. But don't despair. There's always hope.

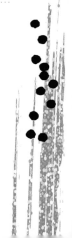

135

Day 60

>>>>———————→

WE ALL FAIL

See what kind of love the Father has given to us, that
we should be called children of God; and so we are.

—1 JOHN 3:1 ESV

I'm sorry if I'm the first to tell you this, but brave or not, you *are* going to fail. We all fail. Failure is a part of every person's life. Just ask a friend or a grown-up about the last time they failed—we all have those stories! But failing doesn't make you a failure. It's when we let it define us that things go wrong. Brave kids don't let failure define them or tell them who they are; they let failure teach them, knowing that God loves them no matter what. Next time you mess up, be brave enough to admit it and brave enough to try again!

When is one time that you failed at something?

....

....

....

....

....

....

.... When you know who loves

.... you, you know where you

.... can go when you fail.

....

....

....

....

....

Brave people know that they can fail and nothing will change between them and their Father.

Day 61

>>>>———

DON'T BE AFRAID

So do not fear, for I am with you; do not be dismayed,
for I am your God. I will strengthen you and help you; I
will uphold you with my righteous right hand.

—ISAIAH 41:10 NIV

Maybe it's when the lights go out at night or maybe it is when
there is a thunderstorm or maybe when you are sitting alone
at the lunch table—any and all of those things might make you
feel afraid. But God reminds us over and over in the Bible to not be
afraid—"DO NOT FEAR," He says. So even in those scary moments,
from the ones that scare lots of people (like a national emergency or
natural disaster) to the ones that just scare you (like a sound in the
middle of the night), be brave. Remind yourself that God is with you,

that you are NEVER alone, and that fear is a liar! Fear is trying to tell you that you are alone—you aren't!

What makes you feel afraid right now? How does it help to know that God is with you?

....
....
....
....
....
....
....

> When we take steps forward, we've got to say no to fear.

....
....
....
....
....
....

Please don't let fear win.

Day 62

FACE YOUR PAIN

Even though I walk through the valley of the shadow of death, I will fear no evil, for you are with me; your rod and your staff, they comfort me.

—PSALM 23:4 ESV

Sometimes we hide the things that scare us or hurt us—like a cut on our hand or an embarrassing moment at school. But brave kids don't run from what hurts them—they face their pain. It's better when you say the thing that hurts out loud. That's brave. Telling someone about your pain, whether it's lies the enemy plants in your head or a very sad circumstance you're wading through, is brave. When you face the pain—look at it and call it what it is—you will begin to experience healing. Hiding it doesn't lead to healing. Especially if someone else hurt your feelings or your body, hiding it will not help it get better. Face the pain and let the secret out.

What pain is weighing you down right now?

....
....
....
....
....
....
....

> Face your pain. Bring it to God. Share it with another person and find healing there.

....
....
....
....
....

Friend, are you hurting?
Don't run from it.

Day 63

>>>> ──────→

INVITE SOMEONE
INTO YOUR PAIN

You can't whitewash your sins and get by with it; you
find mercy by admitting and leaving them.

—PROVERBS 28:13 MSG

Sin and pain love a good secret. You've got to be brave to tell that
embarrassing or sad story to the people who love you. You may be
worried they will stop caring for you if they know. But just try it,
and you'll be surprised. You'll be surprised how often people give grace.
You'll be surprised at how quickly the light eliminates the darkness, and
despite what your mind tells you, you will feel braver once it's out in the
open. Safe adults and safe friends will stand by you and help you heal
from the pain you are feeling today. Don't hide it anymore.

Are you carrying shame over a certain sin or experience? Write about it and plan to share it with someone.

....

....

....

....

....

....

....

> The darkness can't hang around when it's exposed in the light.

....

....

....

....

....

....

Don't keep secrets. Tell somebody you trust. Please.

Day 64

FIND A SAFE PERSON

Walk with the wise and become wise, for a companion
of fools suffers harm.

—PROVERBS 13:20 NIV

as anyone ever been unkind to you? Hurt your feelings or hurt your
body? Have they told you to keep it a secret or have you kept it a
secret because you feel ashamed? It takes a lot of courage to find
a safe adult—maybe a parent, teacher, pastor, or coach—and be brave
enough to tell them you have been hurt. What happened is not your
fault, and it didn't happen because you deserve to be hurt—a safe adult
will remind you of all these things. But it is so important to be brave in
this way. Even if one of your friends has asked you to keep a secret of
how someone hurt them, you can be brave and tell a safe person in your
life. Many adults in your life would love to help you figure out how to

love God, love others, and love yourself. Invite people in and learn from their wisdom and tell them the truth.

Who is a safe adult for you?

....

....

....

....

....

....

> It takes bravery to tell someone when you have been hurt.

....

....

....

....

....

When you know who loves you, you know your safe places.

145

Day 65

>>>> ————

DIVINE DETOURS

Many are the plans in a person's heart, but it is the
Lord's purpose that prevails.

—PROVERBS 19:21 NIV

Have you ever noticed when your parents have to take a different road home because the normal road is closed? Or maybe you have to walk a different path in the park because the normal path is being repaired? These are called detours, and they happen all the time in our real lives and in our spiritual lives too. The ones that God sets up I call divine detours. Usually, divine detours are no fun in the moment because they change the plan you have for what happens next. Whether they involve school, sports, performing arts, friendships, church, or family, they're a shock. They're a change in plans that you didn't ask for. But they take us where we're supposed to go in the long run—so you get to be brave and trust in the story that God is writing in your life, even when it takes a surprise turn!

What is a plan in your life that has changed suddenly?

....

....

....

....

....

| A divine detour may just be God's way of getting you to look up at Him. |

....

....

....

....

....

....

....

God sees the whole picture.
You can trust Him, even when
He derails your plan.

Day 66

>>>———➤

WHY PERSEVERANCE MATTERS

Not only so, but we also glory in our sufferings,
because we know that suffering produces
perseverance; perseverance, character; and character,
hope. And hope does not put us to shame, because
God's love has been poured out into our hearts through
the Holy Spirit, who has been given to us.

—ROMANS 5:3–5 NIV

It is easy for me to quit when something gets hard, like when I am jog-
ging around my neighborhood. But if I want my muscles to build and
my body to be healthy, I have to keep going. I'm learning that courage
builds when I persevere. Like the Scripture verses say above, brave kids

realize that we can rejoice in our sufferings because they grow perseverance in us, and perseverance produces good character, and ultimately, it brings us to the hope we have in Jesus. And hope is worth fighting for.

Is there something you're ready to walk away from? Do you think it would be better to persevere? Why or why not?

....
....
....
....
....
....
....

Hold on. Persevere.

....
....
....
....
....

Brave people don't give up.

Day 67

DON'T GIVE UP

Let us not become weary in doing good, for at the
proper time we will reap a harvest if we do not give up.

—GALATIANS 6:9 NIV

O kay, I'm going to tell you something, and I want you to listen.
Don't give up. Don't quit! You're on a journey. You're looking for
brave. You've been looking at your life—at your pain and joys and
experiences—and you've been finding the brave. But don't quit now.
Looking for brave and doing things that are healthy for your mind, body,
and soul will reap a harvest of blessing. That just means that being brave
is like planting seeds, and the fruit that grows from those seeds are
blessings in your life. Think about your life—in your home and in your
school and in your church and in your neighborhood—and think about
all the brave times you decided to keep going instead of giving up. All of

those are so important, and they put you on the path to make the best next decision!

Now that you're more than halfway through this journey of one hundred days, how have you seen bravery show up in your life, heart, or attitude since you began?

....
....
....
....
....
....

Don't quit trying to find the brave in your life.

....
....
....
....
....

Looking for brave will reap a harvest of blessing.

Day 68

WHEN PAIN HEALS

On hearing this, Jesus said, "It is not the healthy who need a doctor, but the sick."

—MATTHEW 9:12 NIV

Sounds crazy, doesn't it? To think that our pain could actually help heal us? But it's true! Our God is a healer. And there are times when God is going to take you through surgery (that could mean a doctor doing REAL surgery on your body or God just doing work on your heart and in your mind and in your life!), not because He wants to hurt you but because He loves you and wants to heal you. I've seen it in my own life—things being cut away, sins being revealed, secrets being exposed, all for my good. When we remember that we're sinners in need of Jesus, we can trust our Great Physician. Of course, it might feel scary to see your life changing, but it's also amazing! God is doing a good work in you!

When has God taken you through something painful in order to help you? How did your life change for the better? (It always does with God!)

....

....

....

....

....

....

> We can be brave in the face of brokenness and pain and spiritual surgery because we know that God is good.

....

....

....

....

Surgery hurts, but it is always for our good and for our health.

brave KIDS
TAKE CARE OF THEMSELVES AND HELP OTHER PEOPLE!

Day 69

GOD'S PURPOSE FOR YOUR BODY

Or do you not know that your body is a temple of the Holy Spirit within you, whom you have from God? You are not your own.

—1 CORINTHIANS 6:19 ESV

Your body, from the way you are shaped to your exact number of fingers and toes, is God's big and best plan for you! And even if you're not able to do everything your friends can do, there's something about your body and what it *can* do that makes you special. That's because God has a purpose for your body—in all its imperfections and differences. He wants to use you, as you are, to show people how great it is to be God's child. Brave kids look at the bodies they are in and choose to see them for what they are—vessels that hold a mighty God and are loved deeply by God the Creator.

How do you feel about your body? How does the way you feel change when you realize your body is home to God's Spirit?

....

....

....

....

....

....

By God's grace, I've gone from thinking my body is never good enough to believing it's a temple of the Holy Spirit.

....

....

....

....

Your health matters because only a working body can be a brave body.

157

Day 70

>>>>————➤

RHYTHMS OF DISCIPLINE

For the moment all discipline seems painful rather than pleasant, but later it yields the peaceful fruit of righteousness to those who have been trained by it.

—HEBREWS 12:11 ESV

*D*iscipline isn't a very fun word, I know. So let's talk more about rhythms, like when a drum beats over and over and makes a rhythm. That rhythm really helps the rest of the instruments play together well. Your discipline, the rhythm that makes you the best you, shows up when it is time to say the right thing, do the right thing, be the brave person you want to be. And when you're brave enough to have good rhythms in your life—like reading your Bible every day, exercising, getting plenty of sleep—they will all work together to make you as healthy as possible and keep your heart strong and full of courage. I often label discipline as something boring and unnecessary, when really discipline is the work done on the practice field so you are ready for the big game.

What are your rhythms of discipline, the things you do to train your body, mind, or spirit? What do you want to add to your routine?

....

....

....

....

....

....

| If you want to be brave, you have to practice.

....

....

....

....

Practice makes perfect, and practice makes you brave.

Day 71

PLEASE PLAY

This is the day that the LORD has made; let us rejoice and be glad in it.

—PSALM 118:24 ESV

I bet this one is maybe the easiest of all one hundred days for you! BRAVE KIDS LOVE TO PLAY. Grown-ups have a hard time with playing sometimes because grown-ups feel like it's not a good use of time. But you know better! You know how much you love to play—just keep doing it! Inside or outside, alone or with friends, a soccer game or a board game, a race or a puzzle, brave kids (and brave grown-ups!) know it is okay and GOOD to play. So keep on doing what you are doing, and when you think you should quit playing, remind yourself how brave it is to play!

What do you like to do for fun? What can you do to break up your day with play?

....

....

....

....

....

....

....

....

> Play is like a deep breath on a really hard journey of courage.

....

....

....

....

....

....

You can have fun and laugh because God is in control.

Day 72

PLEASE EXERCISE

I appeal to you therefore, brothers, by the mercies of
God, to present your bodies as a living sacrifice, holy
and acceptable to God, which is your spiritual worship.

—ROMANS 12:1 ESV

Move your body, my friend! Your bones, muscles, joints, and organs all work together to help you exercise and get stronger. A lifestyle of daily exercise is not about losing weight. It's not a size conversation—your body doesn't have to be tiny or huge. It's about another way to worship God—with your body! It's about honoring your body and treating it well. Your body was meant to move; it was not meant to be still. Why? Because you need your whole body to be strong enough to do all the things you were called to do for as many years as possible.

What's your exercise routine? How can you make this time an act of play and of worship?

....
....
....
....
....
....
....
....

Just get out there and move your body.

....
....
....
....
....
....
....
....

Your body is a temple of God that you get to use for His glory.

Day 73

PLEASE EAT YOUR VEGGIES

So, whether you eat or drink, or whatever you do, do
all to the glory of God.

—1 CORINTHIANS 10:31 ESV

know this sounds crazy, but actually it's true! Brave kids eat their
veggies whenever they get the chance! I'm not saying you can never
eat the burger. Burgers are fantastic, but if you thoughtlessly eat food
that tastes good and fail to eat food that is actually good for you, you are
not treating your body well. God has given your body to you for a reason.
He has a purpose for your life. And vegetables do so many good things
for your muscles and organs, and the world needs your brave brain and

heart to be strong and healthy. So next time you don't want to try a new vegetable on the plate, remind yourself how brave you are and try a bite!

What is one vegetable you like to eat?

....
....
....
....
....
....
....
.... Moderation is key, friends.
....
....
....
....
....

Be thoughtful. Take care of this gift that is your body.

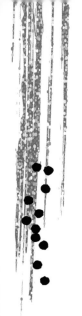

Day 74

PLEASE REST

It's useless to rise early and go to bed late, and work
your worried fingers to the bone. Don't you know he
enjoys giving rest to those he loves?

—PSALM 127:2 MSG

Remember when you were a little kid and you took naps every day? That doesn't happen anymore, right? But sleep makes you healthy. Our bodies are meant for rest. Even God rested when He created the world, remember? So when you lie down in bed at night, don't play in your room or read for hours (that's what always gets me in trouble— GOOD BOOKS!) or play video games—all things that will keep you awake and steal your sleep. If our goal is to be brave, then we have to be well rested too. So take naps when you want, especially when your body is growing and changing, and get good sleep every night!

What is your favorite thing to do at night when it's time to get ready for bed?

....
....
....
....
....
....
....

> Brave people recognize
> that there are times
> when you have to stop.

....
....
....
....
....
....
....

*Be brave enough to rest knowing
that you need it, that it's healthy.*

Day 75

SABBATH

"Do your work in six days and rest on the seventh day."

—EXODUS 34:21 CEV

In the Bible, there is one day a week when families rest together. God did it when He created the world, and Jesus practiced it too—it's called "Sabbath." Sometimes every day feels busy, doesn't it? But having a day of rest—when you don't do homework or chores and just rest and worship—is really important! Brave friends, please choose to have a Sabbath. Unplug from your tablet. Give yourself a break from schoolwork. Say yes to rest and yes to relationships. Sabbath is something we are called to—a discipline that will make our lives better if we embrace it.

Describe what a day of rest and worship looks like to you. When can you take a Sabbath this week?

....
....
....
....
....
....
....
....
....

You've got to take time away from the things that keep you busy. Regularly.

....
....
....
....
....
....
....
....

We need Sabbath. We need rest.

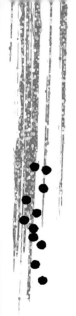

Day 76

WORDS CAN HEAL

The words of the reckless pierce like swords, but the tongue of the wise brings healing.

—PROVERBS 12:18 NIV

Look at today's verse. Reckless words? They hurt. You know the kind of words that are "reckless"—it means saying something without thinking, and often those things hurt someone else. But words can heal too. Brave kids don't gossip and use their words to hurt others. Brave kids use their words to heal. Speaking with kindness about other people's hearts and minds *and* bodies can go a long way to heal. You can absolutely change someone's day by how you speak to them—so heal someone today by speaking kindly to them!

What words spoken by others have been healing to you?

....

....

....

....

....

....

....

....

We have two options when we use our words: we can build or we can destroy.

....

....

....

....

....

....

....

....

Words. Are. Powerful.
Use yours to build.

HEALTHY KIDS THINK ABOUT OTHER PEOPLE

Jesus replied: "'Love the Lord your God with all your heart and with all your soul and with all your mind.' This is the first and greatest commandment. And the second is like it: 'Love your neighbor as yourself.' All the Law and the Prophets hang on these two commandments."

—MATTHEW 22:37–40 NIV

If you're truly being brave and if you're truly pursuing being a healthy human, you grow to love yourself and you love other people out of that. That's how brave people—kids and adults—spend their lives: loving God, loving others, and loving themselves. (Just look at that scripture!)

To love someone is to believe in *them*. When someone believes in you, it changes everything—how you carry yourself, how you treat others, how you live day after day. You can give that same gift to those around you.

You have to love yourself before you can love others. Do you love yourself now? How can you grow to love yourself more?

....
....
....
....
....
....

> You have to love yourself to love others well.

....
....
....
....
....

Healthy, brave people love other people.

Day 78

>>>———→

BE A LEADER

Follow my example, as I follow the example of Christ.

—1 CORINTHIANS 11:1 NIV

It may not feel natural to you to be the front of the line or to have your classmates or teammates looking at you to lead, but we all get to lead sometimes. The Bible challenges men and women to lead by example—how you treat other people, how you talk to them and about them, and how you make choices. Whether it's a friend at school or a younger sibling or the other kids on your sports team or in the musical, someone is looking up to you and following what you do. How you live is how you lead, and it takes a lot of courage to do that well!

Can you list one person you know you are leading right now? What does it take to be a good leader?

....

....

....

....

....

....

....

> Brave people don't just pour into their own hopes and dreams. They pour their wisdom and time and love into others.

....

....

....

....

....

....

It is life-giving to take what the Lord has taught you and pass it down.

Day 79

BLAZE A TRAIL

Your word is a lamp to my feet and a light to my path.

—PSALM 119:105 ESV

I have a favorite trail here in my town, Nashville, Tennessee. And some-times I think about the first person who ever walked on that trail through the woods. They had to face a lot of obstacles—like tree roots and a creek—but because they went first, I can walk that trail so easily now. You, my friend, are blazing a trail with your life for the younger girls and boys behind you. You are making a way for them, saving them some trouble and hard days by providing a clear path. How you live your life and make decisions, the heart you have for other people—all of that shows others the way to live well.

Who is a leader YOU look to as a trailblazer?

....
....
....
....
....
....
....
....
....

We all need trailblazers.

....
....
....
....
....
....
....

Never forget that you are a trailblazer.

Day 80

EVERYTHING YOU
HAVE IS GOD'S

The earth and everything on it belong to the LORD. The
world and its people belong to him.

—PSALM 24:1 CEV

A good and brave lesson to carry through your whole life is that
everything you have is God's. He has given you so many good
things—it's your job to care for them! God gives us a new identity
in Christ. Now we are His, and we are stewards, or caretakers, of His
stuff. So your time, your money, all your talents, even your story—it's
God's, my friend. Living with that understanding takes courage because
how we handle all that God has given us takes work and thoughtfulness

and time! Everything you have is God's. So be brave enough to steward everything you have in a way that displays God's greatest generosity.

What does it look like to live like everything you have is God's?

....

....

....

....

....

....

....

> Living for yourself? That's easy. Living like everything you have is God's (because it is)? That's brave.

....

....

....

....

....

Are you brave enough to believe God has been generous to you?

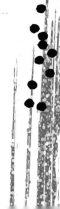

Day 81

>>>> ———→

BE GENEROUS WITH YOUR TIME

Share with the Lord's people who are in need. Practice hospitality.

—ROMANS 12:13 NIV

There are days when it feels like we are wasting time—like when we have to do something we don't like or be with people we don't like or study something in school that is boring. It's not easy to give your time to God and others. I get that. It's way more fun to DO WHAT YOU WANT TO DO! And a lot of times we get to do that. But serving other people, helping your parents with chores, talking to your neighbor, whatever it is—that time is precious and that time is sacred. Other people will experience God's love when you give them your time.

Are you brave enough to be generous with your time, trusting that God has a purpose in it?

Name one person you love talking with. How can you share your time with them today?

....

....

....

....

....

....

....

> God trusts us to be brave and to be generous with each day He gives us on the planet.

....

....

....

....

The time God has given us was created by Him and belongs to Him.

Day 82

BE GENEROUS WITH WHAT YOU KNOW

If any of you lacks wisdom, let him ask God, who gives generously to all without reproach, and it will be given him.

—JAMES 1:5 ESV

God is so generous with us. He gives good gifts to His children, and wisdom is such an incredible gift. What you already know can help other people so much—whether it is showing a friend how to play a game or sharing a Bible verse you love or helping someone fix a broken item. So this is where your bravery comes in: God has given you a lot of good ideas and a lot of knowledge and wisdom—you know a lot! Brave kids offer help to other people, sharing what they have learned and what they know, to try to make someone else's day easier. Ask God to give you opportunities to share wisdom with others today.

What is one topic you know a lot about?

....

....

....

....

....

....

....

....

....

....

....

....

....

> You are qualified to share godly wisdom because you have God.

He will give you wisdom, and you can give it to others.

Day 83

>>>> ————→

BE GENEROUS WITH
YOUR MONEY

"No one can serve two masters, for either he will hate
the one and love the other, or he will be devoted to the
one and despise the other. You cannot serve God and
money."

—MATTHEW 6:24 ESV

Remember how we said that everything we have belongs to God and He's just asked us to take care of it all? The same is true with money! Money can get complicated because it feels scary to be generous and give it away. But Jesus said you can't serve God and money. It just doesn't work. So we serve God and love God and let money just be a tool in our tool belt to help us do the things we want to do to live for God. Are you using your money in a way that honors Him? It's not easy. I know! But are you brave enough to believe that if you are generous with your money, you won't run out?

What's one way you can be generous with your money today?

....
....
....
....
....
....
....

God blesses us so richly when we are generous.

....
....
....
....
....

God uses our money to spread His love to others.

Day 84

BE GENEROUS WITH YOUR WORDS

Gracious words are like a honeycomb, sweetness to the
soul and health to the body.

—PROVERBS 16:24 ESV

*H*ave you ever been around someone whose words were just mean all the time? We can use our words to hurt others, to be negative, to gossip, and to complain. Or we can be brave enough to step out into a harmful, cynical world, where people want to hear gossip and negativity, and instead we can be generous with our words and use them to bring life. Speak kindly to each other, go out of your way to say something nice to a classmate or teacher, write a note to your family members and tell them why you are thankful for them. Your words matter so much. Don't hold back! Be generous with them!!

What does it mean to "bring life" with your words?

....

....

....

....

....

....

Be different in a world that uses words to hurt. Use your words to heal.

....

....

....

....

....

Be intentional and generous with your words to yourself, to others, and to God.

Day 85

>>>>———→

BE GENEROUS WITH
YOUR STUFF

Make sure you don't take things for granted and go
slack in working for the common good; share what you
have with others. God takes particular pleasure in acts
of worship—a different kind of "sacrifice"—that take
place in kitchen and workplace and on the streets.

—HEBREWS 13:16 MSG

Your books are your books. Your games are your games. Your
sports equipment is your sports equipment. Your instrument is
your instrument. But life is so much better when we share! It
doesn't mean you have to give your things away (though sometimes
that's exactly what you should do!), but letting other friends use your

things is a brave move, a sign of trust. It builds good generosity muscles in us to share the things that are most important to us. Be the first to share, and watch as your friends and siblings follow your lead and share their things with you too!

What is one thing you can share today? What are some feelings you experience when you share?

....
....
....
....
....
....

Be brave enough to love
the people around you.

....
....
....
....

*Brave people are generous
with what they have.*

Day 86

>>>>———→

ALL YOU HAVE AND
ALL YOU SHARE

Tell them to go after God, who piles on all the riches
we could ever manage—to do good, to be rich in
helping others, to be extravagantly generous. If they do
that, they'll build a treasury that will last, gaining life
that is truly life.

—1 TIMOTHY 6:18–19 MSG

*B*rave kids do their best to think about other people more than they think about themselves. It shows up in how you handle your things and how you share your things—like games and stories and time. Brave kids take what God's given them and give generously. Friend, what you have and who you are should make an impact on this planet. Be brave enough to put yourself, your wants, your money, and your time in second place, so that what you have—what God's given you to steward—makes a difference wherever you go and whoever you are around.

How do you dream of making a bigger and bolder impact one day?

....

....

....

....

....

....

....

....

> All you have and all you share will make a difference in this world— by furthering God's kingdom.

....

....

....

....

Show others the love of
Christ in a tangible way.

brave KiDS
ARE WORLD CHANGERS!

Day 87

SACRED PLACES

"Do not come any closer," God said. "Take off your sandals, for the place where you are standing is holy ground."

—EXODUS 3:5 NIV

Do you know the word *sacred*? It means extra special and it's usually saved for God. So a sacred moment might be a prayer or when you take communion. A sacred place is somewhere special you meet with God. Because we have this amazing access to the Father through Jesus, we can talk to God wherever and whenever, but I think it's really important to have a sacred place with Him too. Maybe it's where you keep your Bible or a favorite spot in your backyard where you sit and think and talk to God. Having a sacred place, especially when you are trying to be brave, feels really special and helps connect with God.

Where is your sacred space, the place where you intentionally spend time with God? How can you make it special for when you sit down to spend time with God?

....
....
....
....
....
....

> You can't expect to be brave without spending time with God.

....
....
....
....
....

Your sacred space doesn't have to be fancy. Just find a spot and make it sacred.

Day 88

>>>———→

BE RIGHT WHERE
YOU ARE

"My command is this: Love each other as I have
loved you."

—JOHN 15:12 NIV

Wherever you live, wherever you go to school, wherever you hang out, be all there. For me to do that, I have to put my phone down sometimes. Maybe for you it's putting down your tablet or book, or maybe it's sitting in the kitchen with your parents while they cook dinner. But instead of being distracted by a lot of things, can you practice being focused on one thing or one conversation? Loving others means being present with them in their pain and their joy. It means being all there.

What's one way you can be present this week?

....
....
....
....
....
....
....
....
....

Are you brave enough to believe that you're not missing out on something else?

....
....
....
....
....
....

Be intentional about being present where you are.

Day 89

WHERE YOU MEET
WITH GOD

Let the heavens rejoice, let the earth be glad; let the sea
resound, and all that is in it. Let the fields be jubilant,
and everything in them; let all the trees of the forest
sing for joy.

—PSALM 96:11–12 NIV

love being outside. Do you? Even when it's hot, even when it's cold, I
love seeing the trees and the animals and watching them all change as
the year passes. Spending time in God's creation, in His presence, will
make you brave because it reminds you that you're God's. Today, even if
it's just going outside for a few minutes and sitting under a tree, spend

time in creation and remember how loved you are and how brave you can be. Nature is one of the places that it feels easy to meet with God.

Where will you go to spend time in God's creation today?

....
....
....
....
....
....
....

His love makes me brave, and there is no place I love to meet with God more than sitting in His creation.

....
....
....
....
....

Just sit. Just be. Sometimes the Lord just wants to hang out.

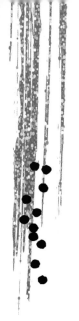

Day 90

>>>>———

WHERE YOU LIVE

My friends, you were chosen to be free. So don't use
your freedom as an excuse to do anything you want.
Use it as an opportunity to serve each other with love.

—GALATIANS 5:13 CEV

How can you be brave in your home with the people you live with?
Think about the grown-ups and the kids you see every day in your
house. Being brave with your family and the people you live with
really makes a difference! You can unload the dishwasher or play with
your little brother or sister. You can clean up when you make a mess or
tell a secret that you've been holding on to. Where you live should be
a safe place. (If it isn't, please tell a safe adult in your life.) In the places
where you find the most comfort, you have to have a little extra something to give there. I think it's brave.

Who lives in your house with you? Make a list and then add something special you can do with them this week!

....
....
....
....
....
....
....
....

> Home is where we find peace, so to sacrifice in that place is to sacrifice deeply.

....
....
....
....
....
....
....

Courage often looks like sacrifice and service.

Day 91

YOUR NEIGHBORHOOD

"The second [commandment] is this: 'Love your neighbor as yourself.' There is no commandment greater than these."

—MARK 12:31 NIV

Jesus said the second greatest commandment was to love your neighbors. Walk to your front door and look at the houses or apartments around you—those are your neighbors! We can absolutely take this verse to mean all other people too, but, friend, you've got actual neighbors all around you who need to know that hope is found in Jesus. Do you know them? How are you serving them and caring about them? Be brave enough to see the people around you, ask them questions, invite them to play, and share with them—your toys, your stories, your friendship.

How well do you know the people who live around you? What are some ways you can get to know them better?

....
....
....
....
....
....
....

> How is your neighborhood different because you live in it?

....
....
....
....
....
....

Be brave enough to love the people around you. God will use you, friend.

Day 92

YOUR CITY

"Also, seek the peace and prosperity of the city to which I have carried you into exile. Pray to the LORD for it, because if it prospers, you too will prosper."

—JEREMIAH 29:7 NIV

When you think about the puzzle of the person you are, the zip code on your mailing address is an important piece. So what does it look like to love the city you're in? Even if you wish you lived somewhere else right now, even if you're here just for a season, God has placed you in your city for a purpose. It is no accident that your family, or the grown-ups who care about you, brought you to this city. There is a lot for you to learn here and ways to grow. Be brave in your city—visit some parks and make some new friends!

How are you being brave—serving and loving others—in the city where you live now?

....

....

....

....

....

....

....

....

....   It takes courage to serve in new

....   places just down the street.

....

....

....

....

....

....

....

Being brave in your city
means serving.

Day 93

>>>>————→

YOUR COUNTRY

Let every person be subject to the governing authorities.
For there is no authority except from God, and those
that exist have been instituted by God.

—ROMANS 13:1 ESV

There are almost two hundred countries in the WORLD—which one is your home? Have you gotten to visit any other countries? In the country where you live, being brave looks like praying for your leaders, celebrating the best parts of your country, and paying attention to the ways that you can help serve your neighbors and your country. Think of a few reasons you are grateful to live in the country you live in. It may not be perfect, but I bet there is something great. And be brave and dream of some other countries you would like to see!

What do you like about your country? What changes would you like to see made?

....
....
....
....
....
....
....
....

> No matter what the political state of things may be, you can be brave.

....
....
....
....
....

Brave people trust God with who is or isn't in authority over them.

Day 94

THE WORLD

And [Jesus] said to them, "Go into all the world and proclaim the gospel to the whole creation."

—MARK 16:15 ESV

So where in this great big world do you want to travel? If you've never had a moment when no one around you speaks your language or shares your skin tone or knows how elementary school works, you need to go. You need to see that the world is big and diverse, and maybe God doesn't look or sound the way you always thought He did, because the world has a lot of people who look and sound different from you, all of whom are made in His image. If everyone on earth is made in the image of God, then the more neighbors and friends you meet from around the world, the more you'll see all the different people that will remind you of God!

Is there a place outside of your country you'd like to visit? Where and why? How can you be brave there?

....
....
....
....
....
....
....

> If you go where you've never gone before, you will see God like you've never seen Him before.

....
....
....
....
....

You need to see how other places and people view God.

Day 95

>>>> ———➤

JERUSALEM

Pray for the peace of Jerusalem: "May those who love you be secure. May there be peace within your walls and security within your citadels."

—PSALM 122:6-7 NIV

*W*e've talked about the power of prayer, and friend, it is real. Prayer changes things. So when you pray for places like your home and your neighborhood and your city and your country and the world, pray for Jerusalem—it is the *only* city God specifically asks us to pray for. Jerusalem is in Israel, and a lot of the best stories in the Bible took place there—it's where King David and Jesus both spent a lot of their time! And people still live there today. Pray for the citizens and the businesses and the schools and the churches. Pray for safety and peace.

Begin praying for Jerusalem today. Pray for its people and prosperity.

....

....

....

....

....

....

....

....

....

We are asked by God to pray
for the peace of Jerusalem.

....

....

....

....

....

....

....

*Prayer is our most direct connection to
God—your voice straight to His ear.*

brave KIDS

BRAVE KIDS FINISH
WHAT THEY STARTED!

Day 96

JESUS WAS BRAVE

"If the world hates you, keep in mind that it hated me first."

—JOHN 15:18 NIV

Jesus was brave. It makes me feel more courage in my heart remembering that Jesus did some majorly brave things right here—right where we are. He was human like you and me. He was tempted to make mistakes like you and me. And He took a risk on you and me. He asked His disciples to do the same. To give up everything to follow Him. To live bravely, as He did—pouring out His life for a hurting, hostile world. Remembering how brave Jesus was in His life can help us be brave in our lives too!

What are some of your favorite brave things Jesus did on earth?

....

....

....

....

....

....

The world hated Jesus, but He was brave enough to give His life for it anyway.

....

....

....

....

....

....

....

The Son of God came to do the most courageous thing this planet has ever seen.

Day 97

JESUS IS BRAVE

Then I saw heaven opened, and behold, a white horse!
The one sitting on it is called Faithful and True.

—REVELATION 19:11 ESV

Jesus was brave on earth, but He is alive and well! John 3:16 says it all. God is holy and we are sinners. But Jesus bridged that gap between us and God; His death and resurrection cleared that path. And one day Jesus is coming back, not as the baby in the humble manger but as the mighty King of kings and Lord of lords. He deeply loves you and deeply knows you. Even when we make mistakes over and over again, He forgives. Jesus is brave, and He made you to be brave too.

How does bravery help you carry on Jesus's work?

....
....
....
....
....
....
....
....
....
....

> Jesus is still alive and still
> working for our good today.

....
....
....
....
....
....
....

Jesus wasn't just brave in the past tense. Jesus is brave today.

Day 98

YOU WERE MADE TO BE BRAVE

Then David said to Solomon his son, "Be strong and courageous and do it. Do not be afraid and do not be dismayed, for the LORD God, even my God, is with you. He will not leave you or forsake you, until all the work for the service of the house of the LORD is finished."

—1 CHRONICLES 28:20 ESV

*C*ourage isn't just for mighty warriors. It isn't just for grown-ups. It isn't just for other kids. It's for you. It's for your relationship with God. It's for your dreams and your friendships and your hopes for your future. You can be brave during all the changes of life—and there are a lot to come in your family, in your body, in your brain, and in your life. You can be brave in the face of pain. You can be brave with your health. Brave with your money. Brave wherever you are!

When you look back at the time you've spent over the last ninety-eight devotionals and in God's Word, how do you see that you are braver?

....

....

....

....

....

> There is not an area of your life that can't be touched and improved by courage.

....

....

....

....

....

....

Your God will not leave you. And because you know that, you are brave.

Day 99

YOU ARE BRAVE

Take a good look at God's wonders—they'll take your breath away.

—PSALM 66:5 MSG

When you started this one-hundred-day journey, I bet you were challenging yourself, taking brave steps, and all the while feeling a little bit afraid. But flip through these pages and look at how brave you are—it's amazing! Take this day to reflect on the awesome miracles God has performed for you and in you and in the people around you—like your friends and family. Your brave choices have ripple effects, like when you toss a pebble into a pond. Brave people inspire those around them to be brave—I bet your courage has inspired people that you love!

What has God done in you and through you to show that you are brave?

....
....
....
....
....
....
....
....
....

Do you see now that you are braver than you know?

....
....
....
....
....
....

All glory for any bravery we exhibit goes straight to Jesus.

Day 100

LET'S ALL BE BRAVE

"The LORD your God is with you, the Mighty Warrior who saves. He will take great delight in you; in his love he will no longer rebuke you, but will rejoice over you with singing."

—ZEPHANIAH 3:17 NIV

*F*riend, let's ALL be brave! It will make such a difference for your whole life if you make courage a big part of who you are. In fact, making brave choices in your life is going to change the world. At the least, it will change *your* world. But I dare not limit what you are going to do on this planet, friend. Your life is Jesus's reward for His suffering—your brave yeses, your courageous nos, all of it. Today, as we finish together, remember you are NOT too young to be brave! Start now! I pray courage for you—the deep, deep kind that changes the way